BLUE HORSE of MORNING

For Roger, with love

BLUE HORSE of MORNING

ROSE FLINT

SEREN BOOKS

SEREN BOOKS is the book imprint of
Poetry Wales Press Ltd
Andmar House, Tondu Road
Bridgend, Mid-Glamorgan

British Library Cataloguing in Publication Data
Flint, Rose
Blue Horse of Morning.
I. Title
821.914

ISBN 1-85411-053-5

The publisher acknowledges the financial support of the Welsh Arts Council

Typeset in 10.5 point Palatino by Megaron, Cardiff
Printed by John Penry Press, Swansea

Cover Art: Die grossen blauen Pferde (Large Blue Horses), 1911, by Franz Marc, courtesy of the Walker Art Center, Minneapolis, USA.

CONTENTS

MORNING YOGA FOR THOSE WITH LIMTED TIME

Joy in the cat-stretch; observe how the movements
imitate the waking feline of your house.
In mornings of limited time, this asana
brings the body cleanly away from sleep.

Stand; lean down to place your palms upon the mat.
Breathe the precious air slowly, limbs straight,
your chin tucked close as you stare at your ankles.
This is the first position, nerves strung into place.
So the jungle cats were seen to flex and stretch
under the sun-shadowed temple leaves.

With a sweeping circular motion bring your head down
and forward through the arch of your elbows,
your heart low to the earth. Using the taut strength
of your straightening arms push your spine upward,
backwards – This is the curve of the Cobra
rising sleek as a bow over the temple stones
to gaze and gaze at the sky.

Return to the first position.
Perform five slow downward sweeps.
You are not yet as fine-tuned as the cat
who needs but one lithe gesture
to link her body with Heaven.

IN WAKING

In waking my skin held a different life,
it wanted: flickering
it slid out of sleep   the cells of it
sharp as diamond   pin-points of light.
It muscled: arousal   rippled to corners
of little stiff finger, toe, slanting eyelid
filling and swelling the peony of mouth line
glossy knee hollow.   Snake-skin
shuked over me, perfume of Indies risky as spice
scenting the stinging flames   stroking
        this splendid tissue holding me
pouring its blazing senses into the leaky spaces
        of eyes   mouth   sex
you inside me   I inside out.

How we exchange, know each other more
        in this metamorphosis:
you with your day-sails
driven inward to the flood of black oceans
and I   cave of furled colours
dancing outside   as if
I was light   poured over the wave.

THORNROSE

(Sleeping Beauty)

The valley won't breathe every day;
the air holds to the ground
something stubborn, angry,
gets you round the throat in this mood,
the hood of fogged rain on the hill
goes under your collar
in a scarf of misery. You the somnambulist
setting the pails, battering ice
as the dark lurches about
slips out of your frozen gloves.

Winter tightening the knot in your stomach
that pulses: *Let me out*
Out of this valley of thick thorn walls
that rear so ominously
(seasons of hot blood on the sticks)
and the trees that yowl
cold wolf-sibilants under the doors
in through the chinks –
the curtains tremor.
Sometimes
flood cuts you off, or snow.
Did you know that silence can kill
as it clogs in the veins
mutes the lanes and your mouth?

But the other face of the valley
is sloe blue with earliness, pearl
sky at peace over the lambing,
the creatures' warm push in your hands.

Listen! Larks beginning;
their far voices fracturing hyaline air
into softness.
The sun illuminates.
The spindle-tree trembles with halo.
How can you leave? Cannot leave this valley
where black thickets will quicken white flowers
sudd on the wind through the seemly halls
of your housewifing.
Here you can dream
on the perfume and vision, float
flaxen hair high in the utmost leaves,
body's long curves
rephrasing the hillside.
Anticipating:
for these green walls have a trick
of parting, to let the prince in.

BLUE HORSE OF MORNING

If I came to you now
on the blue horse of morning
how I would cackle the street bells
and set the ghosts groaning out of the light.
I could come as Cloud-Woman-Riding
shape myself into a message
over your roof. *Look, it is dawn,*
the winter is over, wanting is finished.
I have galloped the night-iron out
of our hooves. Accept this silver:
four bright moony hoops flung over the pole.

I could be cool, responding
to weathermen's turquoise oracles,
blue as the inside flame is blue.
You would know me as Ocean, lapping
your island back, fire-blue tiding up
through your heels to break kisses,
sparks over your neck, leave wet shadows.

Or choosing the warmth of lapis lazuli,
I would enter your dark troubled sleep
and thief-silent, go down to the place
where the black root twists darkness
into your dreams. Spreading the rustle
of indigo skirts I would open your mouth
with my long scented fingers
and place the sun on your tongue.

SOMETIME ELECTRIC HOUSE

Without you, this feeling:
boxed in   negative
walls shunt inward and I
                    bang about, hurtle
from one surface to another.
I am spider-haired   so spiky
          angers could nearly ignite me.
My static frightens
the frail pierced-oak staircase
the tinderous worm-nibbled cupboards.

With you, House lazes out
drapes down the sensitive brittled curtains,
pomades tables, chairs to satinwood.
Your presence   balancing mine:
firecat, bluebird, brown-eyed child
humming   music of fusion.
               Our electric harmony
touching sparks   setting powers.

NEEDS OF THE BONE

In pearled firstlight and shadows
my tawny cat comes to wrap his loving
grass-scent fur around my sleep,
prints lace with nettle-trails,
the stitch of finished rain.
He comes to me out of the hill's long quiver,
polishes his tameness with pink quick tongue.

Last night a vixen's eerie woman-voiced singing;
the hens still tremble.
I'd make you a collar out of her pelt, Joe said.
Sensuous, luxurious, warm against even Siberian winters .
Imagine it: chimed black air's rush
over snowfields, tossed furs rich in the troika
frost gemming each separate hair;
the cold smoke of your breath,
fox at your smooth naked throat.

How he sees me –
in the skin of another creature:
animal mouth fit for a kiss on the wind,
the threat and war, the pleasure of savagery.
He'd have me under him in a dress of wildness
to prove his mastery over my kith and kin
with their claws, curved horns, hooves, yellow eyes –
their evasive, magical laws of flight and secrecy.

I've seen dog-fox and vixen playing like cats
on a diamond lawn, coiling long sable bodies
each in the ring of the other, calling
their own winter's tune: the needs of the bone.
I would as soon wear my cat's empty coat

as fold soft fox to my shoulders,
I and the cat and the vixen
share the same fall of the moon,
groundswell, the delicate tightness of space.

In the deep bone of winter my need:
for a meeting place between fire and the frozen river,
to lie looped, touch to your touch, eyes shining,
skin-heat igniting the pulse
of the snow-sheeted bed, our mouth-music
springing leaves and miraculous flowers
out of the bare branchy canopy.

THE RETURN OF THE MOTH

The moths have returned.
Out of the shuttered clay
they come dizzying; pallor of wings
whirr and creep on the slide of night glass,
eyes stud garnets desirous
to sip at our spill of light,
our spice room of fatal gold nutmeg.
Later, in May, the window glass
will clack and clatter with black Maybugs
hurling wing-jacket bodies,
urgent and careless
of thorax or precision filaments.

I am drunk with the moon's insect humming
the flare of sharp night-scent
new bulbs flower-swelling.
I could open this slit of a window
enter the vine, climb
down hand over hand, call you out:
Moth, Mothman –
the garden bending oak darkness over me;
my white body cold-grained as sugar
or salt, your old black coat
covering naked flame.

OUT OF KILTER

What my body told my head was
    random weight: the soft tongue
without speech between us;
the length   flowing as stem to globe – this
only a sketch,   or gesture,
  as if air blew vents between
each gram — *I could be glass* — or
  audible shiver.

                Knowing only
      the hot shell of your mouth
there, in that place, inside,
  a little to the left.
          A shifted, unkiltering centre.

ECLIPTIC

– the yearly path of the Sun through the Heavens

In the season's turnaround, sun's long slant
touching the colours of wheatstraw
and furrow into ripened yellowness,
we met our ghosts-selves, young
and empty-handed under the orchard russets.

Gathering damsons – that glowing month:
you reaching up from the red car's roof
solar god in the gold
leaf brilliance – such plenty :
nightblue fruit wealth on the tongue.
I had hurt with the shock of you,
new, unimagined, generous.

Now this warm October: you
and the sapling boy, his smallness
curves to the bole of a may
while you climb, pose where gilding burnishes
leaf's coin on the slope and edges
of ribcage, shoulders, grace
that you bring
light on the bloom
of midnight's ecliptic bed.
The sudden shock of you, gleaming
and smiling, shining,
Midas-touching me rich.

That ghost-girl-self: *sootfall of hair,*
Indian cheekbones and nerves
green wire, strung bryony.
She must have seen us – even fleetingly –

in the long shadow of trees,
the disc of honey.
You and I here, our gold-ringed hands
brimming:
our older bodies ivy, berried holly.

FROM BLACK BERRIES, BITTERSWEET

She is whiteness, damask for his banquets.
Her willing hands floss sugar,   sculpt
ice into swans   melting with love;
she is all calm, haven-water, easy under
his swift energies of dark thousand-angers
branch   whirling seed.

Her dreams are loping through forests
unsettling the stinging flare of herbs
feast to her animal senses.   She is wolf-head
muscle-lean   black as shulamite
her eyes vermilion.   He is there
in the alders dark sinuous beckoning,
he is there in each tremorous leaf.
If she finds him she will eat
he will eat   out of her hand.
He is olive, scorzonera, sweet dusty carob.

Waking, she lies red on blanched sheets
her dog-days beginning   wolf
thawing from cheekbones   white even teeth.
He sleeps, wine still stretched in his throat
black sloes bitter juice
dissolving his bones into dreams of white waters.
Trees peer in through the window   watch them
curve in together, drowsing spoons;
leaves first stipple of light licking
their skins to awareness.
They will mate soon
go in deep, plunging to love like wolves.

BRAZEN MARRIAGE

After their love had brimmed the bed
and they had floated – dragonflies drowned
in their own heady amber – after he drowsed
into the tasselled cambric, her safe breasts
soft to his nuzzle and her long luxury of pliant bone
unrolled and owned by his momentary hands:
while he lay, a sleek curl in her stroking, netting fingers–
after that, she left him; slipped naked out of the sheets
to kneel on the Chinese ottoman under the window,
crushing dragon blooms of silk, fades of mandarin blossom.

On the other side of the glass
she watches the angels cluster, drift slowly down the hedgerow
through dusk or moonlight; their feet not quite touching
– or risking – the sharpness of quickthorn, mealy plum.
Recently their silvers have flushed to a faint hectic warmth
and one amongst them glistens, has taken the tint of soft metal,
red-gold or bronze. That was after she had lain differently,
her legs gentle hooks, the scarp of her husband's shoulders
a steep rapturous falling.

This angel: his palms push down the light,
his half-skirts rustle impatiently, his penis – meek yet –
stirs in its golden skin. If this Lucifer
clapped his vast and brazen wings
the whole garden would shimmer and dance:
the wind of his feathers husking through oboes,
charming snakes. At his wish, English trees
would fruit with figs and pomegranates and the little foxes
find a sudden banquet of honeyed grapes to lick.
The kingfishers, bird and birdwife, would burn
blue flame down the darts of his eyes.

Turning back to the bed, she sees her husband's body lying
open.
She trails her hands through the texture of his skin
feels his skin flow under and round her like waters,
senses its tensions, muscular wave motions.
Swimming in him, she lets him close over her head,
take her breathless, air becoming wine.
Watching her, his eyes go dark as water from earth-deep
as if she leaned into his eyes, the light behind her.
His body warms her garden scents and rain;
as her reflection fades from the glass.

MESSAGES OF SLEEP

In this cave
darkness battens senses, plays nerve strings,
light's absence thickening over the skin.
Stars carbon into bodies – I am light
I say quickly,
thrusting some speck of unlight out,
going down in flames.

Enough to call you.
And when you come to me
you are the sand-leopard from kingly Assyria
the sand flooding in with you
white and shell-powdered with sea-creatures,
drowsy with jasmine, with cardomom and amber.

How huge your breath.

I stroke your warmth and your heaviness
listen to the messages
of your rhythmic sleep.
I paint them over the darkness,
until they hang glassy translucent colours
across the black sky desert,
across the rock blackness of my walls,
across the darkness of my breasts and eyes.

One thought has spiraled round my wrist.
The black-gold-banded serpent
lays his head upon my hand.
His eyes are grains of sun.
You watch me as I place his curious mouth
between my open lips of hydromel.

MAP MAKING

Quickly, in air I could describe you,
each fold, curve, how space strokes uneven there.
This description my hands give
to my eyes. I have charted this
in blind night's incendiary darkness,
in cool pearl days stolen from February snow.

But this sharpness,
these bladed words where we collide and fall,
these places set common bruises on our inner skins.
And I mark you, touch for touch,
each angry weal of speech
bites acid into love.
Oh – a map surely, we have etched here?
The shapes of these darknesses
– that one, this one –
they are mines, chasms or
black sucking sands opening before us.

Points of departure:
or references drawn both in braille and script
marked down for futurity's choice.
Within these imperfect eyes lies one whole vision
we two share skills enough for reading signs.
And look
that kiss we printed there
was made of a colour so tender
we were afraid to look down
in dizziness – earth grown so small
a bright global ball at our feet.

YOUR WAY WITH WORDS

Your way with words is the path
to enter me. If you would speak
as if honey
were in your mouth, as if you would
lick me with honey,
I could begin to breathe; if you
held out thoughts such as crystals
their reflections would soothe me,
I am attuned to their vibrations.

Instead your words flail round me
as if they are blind, as if you have forgotten
how to see or tune to me. And I, dumb,
call out: *I'm here. See me. I am here.*
Wanting the feel of your rhythmic tongue
licking me; the words
soft as honey
coming into me.

THE RIGGER'S WIFE

His unaccustomed weight left bruises tattoo-blue
against her skin; he'd said
she was thinner, touching the veins
that ran hyacinth ribbons
under her wrist. His muscles, sinews
now were hard and strong as hawsers.
Watching the early light defining his sleeping shape,
she slowly relearned the familiar lines
of this wedded stranger,
this rare visitor come to her bed.

And lay wondering:
what now of her fragile, defensive structures,
the patterns she'd woven for living alone?
Her life-lines would catch him like cobwebs,
he'd toss and struggle
tearing by accident
or design, his own ropes
flowing out of him
coil on coil; snaring her
with his leashes, plaits
of silk and steel.

In time they'd mesh again,
make a net of love to swing inside.
Until the appointed day when
he'd up and go – and she left hanging.

A breathing space
a sense of floating:
before she picked up the threads.

CARAPACE

Only for that cheval glass eye
would she stand naked, shining the mirror's honesty
over her forty-odd years.
She needs a clear-sighted assessment
of the vulnerable places she must defend
and disguise, for she retains a reputation
for elegance, the stains of beauty.

Still her legs are long and slender but dark stockings
will hide any veins daring to swell under stress.
No sandals, nor bare feet, for her toes
are wedge-shaped, unpretty now.
She dresses in simple clothes with nothing to emphasise
the thickening waist, the generous stomach
where storylines of births and fat months
scar into skin gone slack,
too easy to pinch into tucks and folds, all tension moved
to the ache at the nape of her neck.

The kindness of pearls' lustre
gentles the sharpening planes of her face,
the slow tracking of years, love and care.
She pales out her shadows, pretends to be someone
who once lived in her skin; yet she knows her real self
will keep peeping out, like a thin pokey wrist
from the sleeve of an outgrown coat.

Soon, the visual voice of the mirror warns,
soon you'll not be able to shrug illusions over your head.
Time will creep and catch you, however you cheat and fight,
will slide you into the rattling shape
of an old woman's body of delicate bone.

Yet waking to phials and the day's necessary silk,
she is curious, restless even.
Inside the mirror she watches a moth,
furred and cinereous, emerging
from the brittle restrictive splinters of chrysalis
into the next phase, the brief free element of air.

OUT OF THIS

This house is our hand's language,
our hand-to-mouth, hand-to-heart house,
its wood grown foresty with us,
branching over the doorway's air
we sculpted here, its canopy,
notch and whorl, shielding
our shooting-up, sapling children.

Now the children rush hand-over-hand
down the ladders of ivy
and resins of foreign islands
come smoking out of the fire.
We snuff the air like mariners
trace juniper, lime and muscat. Mornings,
the sea-voice moans in my bedroom shells,
when I lift my exquisite slipper
a blaze of sand pours out of the heel.
Wine in the silver cup shouts of Odysseus.

We carve the ark out of the living room,
curve the seasoned oak from our young
first season, peg the beams into staves
that creak their twisty heart-roots
into the elm board raft beneath us, as the house
boat tilts out of this to the next tide:
you and I hand-in-hand, still handfast.

SYMBIOSIS

Sympathy with whales and all large creatures
caught blundering in places scaled for smallness
– zoo-pools or enclosures of bitty, dragging pieces –
But they are always in tune with their weight
and I flounder, outsize monster
beached on the sand, no kinetic energy dancing
within me. Oh – I am a sylph, thin and neat,
why this bigness, this pushy largeness
in front of me? I can't own
these towering legs nor the round face
like an angry red moon in my glass.

You in there – do you hear this,
how I rail and cry at this peculiar thickening?
If I cup my hands down close
will you speak through the hill
of tight-stretched skin,
put your mouth close, call to me?
Must I take you on trust
for nine months with no word?

Only your growing
uncurling fern in the dark symbiotic cave
of my swelling. Only your heart's knowing
the measure my own heart makes.

HE SAID: 'POETS MUST IGNORE THE PRAM IN THE HALL'

The fire of milk-fever is akin to the burn
of a rope biting your wrist, milk arcs
down into Earth, ties you down,
milk suffuses you like blood.
You are transparent, a flask
white and green as young woodland
and words then are small, close-petalled,
inside-fist size, little-egg size,
grip words, cry words: *milk dream white..*

Later, words leaf into your dreams
and wake you out of sleep, riding the mice
in and out of the rafters, glittering
the cat's blue fur. You find a red horse
with runes stamped on his hooves
and you try to read them, upside down, sideways,
leaning into the rocking warmth of his roans
and combed palominoes. You try to read
the dark mash of tealeaves,
the brass cackle of wheatflakes; you sway
head-heavy, the babies coming off you like canna buds.
Whalesongs lull your afternoon eyelids
drown you back into sleep.

Until Owl whispers your name –

You can almost catch the secrets
that hang in the hazels like prayer-scarfs,
almost hear what the water says
as it prayer-wheels over the stone.
You have the tune of Earth thrumming its weather
in through your reedy bones as you tread

careful as porcelain, steady the infant's tipping steps
on the vibrant see-saw grass: big hands
slaved by their little soft hooks.
They have stolen your tongue with their giggling
kisses learnt in another life, breathed
where your mind might have been;
their breath brims your cortex and arteries
clouds your aura with light.

But Owl whispers insistently and Moon demands
Decipher me yawning her sleepy throat.
Grey as night owls the cats moon-eye you.
Decipher me –
Midnight is blazoned with phrases, a spooring
of light points; *Explain me this,* barks Sirius.
shaking constellations to rainbeads,
running slow opal on glass.
Moon is pearlgreen, white as a lychee,
a subtle mysterious globe in your mouth.
But she turns in her time of black degrees,
dark passion-fruit, sour rinding,
stroking the richness of shadows swimming
quick elvers under the white lighting you.
Her dark *Decipher me* –

Pale babies grow, tap colours of earth, honey-ochres,
rose madder, their running bright-sheaving the corn.
You carve a greenstick doll, walnut-shell
boats for the water, shape clay, bread and clothes,
shed words like onion skins, words peeling out of you,
feeding your children's cuckoo-mouths
the words for *moon blood sky earth fruit*

They are singing –

You remember the whispers: *Decipher me   Explain this*
You skim empty hands through the leaves.
In the bleachy grass and the rattle-fruit flowers
letters adhere to the wingtips of beetles,
pattern the chrysalis horn.
You shake pollens and seeds along with the syllables
collecting what's left
for your box of white owl-nights, for cat conversations.
Then you see how your fists' pale moons
are smudged through with darkness down to the bone,
indelible etching the texture of blood.
This is their gift: a language you did not know.
You rehearse the words slowly, tongue slipping
on newness: *love*   and *fear*
the circles of time   *rapture*   *rebirth*

BLUE FORCE

I could have held you: in wild snow
or sleet even, bulk grey to smother dreams,
but you came fierce and dark as a small hour,
slippery as seal, untwisting the knot
from my new hands, your blue force
driving you out to sea.

There was a suitcase
and in it something speaking, the mouth showed
under the handle.
How could I carry that? Suppose
it had licked or bitten me, touched me
with its tongue of griefs...

Nothing could prevent my running
blind-handed, my legs scrabbling sand –
seven-leagues, an acre, an inch.
But you were beyond so fast so fast,
coming from where? hardly pausing.

I was almost swimming, reaching cerulean.
Each inner tide working the bones
into disjoints and shells, washing flesh
into pink salt fragments, my lost anemone mouth
lipping ghost ripples, the pulse of a heart
in the narrows.

We should have both turned into seals:
selky-woman and quick child in the milky ebb.
The ocean in her slumberous mysteries
would have been as kind
as this roughest winter kissing.

OTHER WOMEN: FEAR TAUGHT, FEAR LEARNED

If I drew her out of my shadows
how would she form? Balsa or brass?
Sleek as the grin of a catfish
or round-bellied and soft music enough
to plunge hands in to the willing heart?

In the tank
the piranahs are waiting in hundreds,
such plump innocents these blonde assassins
with their mad girlish eyes, staring
and waiting, unfocused, slightly quivering.
The water is viscous and sheened
with the scales they shed like hairs.
Hair-brushing fish, hands would glove pearl
and fishes pearl teeth would bite hands
to the total of crimson blood,
the zest of bone's arrangement.

I saw her yesterday, she posed
outside the hotel where the beds twined
their blankets and groaned and groaned
in their little hours, gathering the sleep
into grits and blears. She was quite gold,
slender, perverse smoothness
an ultimate touch delicate crane legs
arched foot moulded to high-heel slipper,
hands, elegant in gesture, pointing down
to her hidden black-dressed vulva.
She is the maid, the server
of silver-plate dreams, of rough banquets.
She has neither eyes nor mouth nor energy of hair.

I watch my mannequin,   would carefully
carve her name into her sealed spaces,
let the black air out: a banshee-yell
to fashion nightmares, make a winding-sheet of sleep.

Beyond the place where the avid fish watch glass
and the girls saunter their golden shoes
through the risky evening waters,
I see the long-skirted woman approaching
flowers streaming garlands out of her mouth.
Her smile matches mine to exact dimensions.

ASCENDING

The way out of the beating was to ascend;
try to sleep in a corner of the ceiling.
Difficult not to look down,
but that was what made you fall.

They told her that:
Don't look down
don't   *look down*

                              whispers
in women's voices.

ROMANTIC DESIRE

If I were utterly hidden
would you search for me?
If I had fled completely,
foxily brushing out tracks
and laying false information –
had so carefully disappeared
I'd left no marks
on virgin snow or sand –
would you still go on searching?

If I had shut myself safe
in a fortified castle
I'd name it my prison;
would keep a watch
on the road
from my narrow stone window.
So perverse;
I would always hope
for your sudden appearance
and the rescue
of real love.

And what would the castle yield
to those who'd come later?
The learned men with their lenses
powerful enough
to probe into history,
what would they find –

the graceful disposition
of a woman's bones
across a window ledge

or air ringing clear blue
above a windswept nest of doves?

NIGHT TERRORS

His head thrown back, dreams rattle him,
words babble out in foreignness,
as if this juddering sleep has dumbed
his mother-tongue. I watch him under moonlight:
will this new dream tilt him
into flickering shadow dioramas,
where his open eyes see demons, genies
that hop their mocks and cold-sweat menaces
across his gentle sky-filled walls?

His dreams roam unsafe fields. He dreams
aloneness, dreams how slight he is,
blown winter-leaf within the cyclone.
He dreams love and a dead child
on the bleak rib of the night-mountain,
comes pattering down the familiar corridor
between sleeps to comfort me; knows
my grey silk grief within his curving arm.

We discuss his visions of heaven.
He sees spirits ascending into further and higher
wheels of fiery light. Sometimes
so casually he tells me supernatural facts
I believe he owns some dolphin knowledge,
gift or angelic grace, prevision.

Blue, beautiful sky, this heatwave morning
mayday drowned in pollen.
We mark again the falling river level,
count the stones new glazed by solar fire.

I dream torrential fearful rains. I dream
of dust and towering sand-sculptures
mimicking the trees. I dream your mountain
sliding deeper into unrimmed darkness,
with no eternal ringing moon to mark its way.
I dream of how the mountain's mute stone arms
were cradled round its burden. I dream
of how you call me, call me –
We are running through the black dissolving night,
the wind is dragon's breath,
the track to home becoming molten as we pass.

YOU CAN DREAM BUFFALOES

Another beginning: the iron lid of morning
shoved over, the roar of animals
in from the black, a mood on the fire
and Sleep trailing after you,
tugging your hurrying clothes – How
do you give that cosy wholemeal motherness,
arms safe as bread and the loving
voice cat-tonguing roughness soothing
the schooldays?   How, when your milky eyes
watch colours bouncing wrong from the walls?

You could be a diver and they are fishes,
bubbling a private language out of their cherry mouths:
guppies, guppies...   The word writes itself,
italics undulating over the table,
scales pearling up from the oak.

And all you want is the bed-tent,
the Navajo dark of yarrow and liquorice,
magical geometry knotting and weaving
the shaman's message of Birdman-to-Mountain,
Snake-Loiter, Elk-Rush.
You can dream buffaloes
on the green, their bulk and thunder,
each delicate hoof neat as a high-heeled shoe.
You can dip in a frond of their curling hair,
go back through it, the cloudy spiral twisting round
into the crown on your first baby's head.
Silence: retracing your love
till it grows big as Alice and puffs you out
on a steaming expletive into the squally kitchen
air fragmented by flying clocks, flasks, clementines –

Words and dream
fluttering over the children in butterfly haloes.

Only the reams, the white ricey reams
knowing where you've just been.
Again? says the Paper.
As just for a moment you find your hand drawing
in charcoal, the line flowing easy, perfectly truthful:
the head of your favourite child.
Again? says the Paper. *Drawing in the dust at the grate?*

GROWING PAINS

Black glass night, my head fragile,
the wire of your crying
reeled me up from a thin broken sleep.
How can you hurt so?
Shushing and stroking, the growing pains
splintering your small stiff legs
and my aching.
Until my sudden hands change,
poured honey warmth into your fissures,
soothing and healing;
and myself in the process too, it seemed.

Now you are tall, sun-haired and silent,
I can't hold you through moonrise
or midnight. The warmth of touch,
that kindness, is tabooed by the distance
you're running, long legs running
past Mother and childhood,
strange tides and secretive races
travelling your senses
bruising your heart;
the ache of them fining me down,
both of us
taking shape from the rasp
of these new growing pains.

My hands hang fire, I can hold out no miracles,
only slide words down the table between us,
let you pick and choose: sugared pills or balm,
each sour medicine of lesson given
with the bitter-sweet honey of love.

LILY, IN A LONG COAT

Lily, in a long coat,
her hair's bright aureole lightening the dusk
as she strides down the lane,
hands pushed hard into pockets,
blue eyes miles away.
If she wanted
she could find seashells locked into stone
or watch the V of geese come homing down
to the watery disc of the old marl-pit.
But these things belong to her Primary books
so long put away. At fourteen
she is enrapt by a world of people,
while I, at forty
wonder at the striations of a snail.

My childish summers
I lay in a green willow tent, the pool's brown edge
in my hands. How could I know
that the cool silky feel of the water
would stay on my palms for life?
For soon the garden shrank to a mere seed
and I was dancing away, the glittering town dust
filling me like lamellar sand in a timer:
a gold strata, blue the mood of slate,
rich neon red for the words and pictures; black grains
blown from the rootless towers.
It was all so much learning, such inches to grow.

Coming back to the land
I never found time to carve out a pool for the children.
They grew too fast
pushing up through the cradling trees

to find where the restless motorway led.
Going to meet Lily, in her long dark coat,
with the quiet fields and indigo clouds holding us small
in the sphere of the hills,
I wonder what I have given her,
here, in the country.
Water, earth, the changing sky all now part of her
wound into her being
by virtue of being here.

GREEK DANCER, WAITING

for Holly

Palms flat to her head-dress, tiered gold
my snow-white daughter   hem scrolled
to her ankle –
                                    I could weigh a trove of amethyst
against the fineness of your dark-wing hair.

Greek, even Cretan, described by the angle of your arm
the degree of poise   Your stillness
is the same   hairsbreadth away from movement
depicted on the frescoed walls, the red-gold vases.
Your lines   dance over air.

                                        What would I write
on your hands' henna?   Charm: and prayer against
all insidious blackness, blackness that comes
leaching   wild spores blurring the gesso.

                                            And the moon as amulet
breastplate   the silver
(colour of snakes) making connections:
woman and earth and sky again, the water
eel-silver   turbulent life-tide.

Kohl on the eye-rim; you learn the dues
of those dresses, thin rippled gauze,
watered silk. Learn your own worth
without comparison: lapis lazuli   above rubies.

Cymbals clash; their energy released over Europe.
The decisive clap of your hands
beating time
your bare heels stamping your inscape
on sand or wood.
Dancing the thread   past Kore, Ariadne,
beyond the labyrinth's eye.

SIXTEEN, SEVENTEEN

Times, they fill the spacious limits of the house
trial running the presences they almost have.
Such sorceresses, these daughters.
They shape-shift: bird-girls go snakey,
eyes sly-lidded, insect lips, their music
cackling the grey weary dust from the mortar,
breaking the bovine cups and inherited china
with their flung hair's coronal,
their skirt's strident electricity.
The kitchen fizzes.
The whole groaning window puffs out its panes
to explosion   and I craning outward
to night-sky see nothing – no dancing daughters –
only two silent sharp lights that speed vertical
urgent, North to magnetic South, with no whisper
to mend the shocked garden.

Pale times, I have seen them slide under doors
in etiolated shadows, old white shoe prints
stepped out flat and exhausted.
And times of such brittle containments
of sorrow: thin glass, thin as the high searing note
stroked from the wineglass rim, glass thin
as the water-spider-house. Water-times when they lay
heads down in the tide's blue water-colour wash.

Such times acceleration. Made time and spare time
they have set the windmills humming
with their glances, sewn energy stitch by stitch
into their sculptured horoscopic coats.
They are such wonders.   They are women.

STEALING THE STRENGTH OF MOTHS

Her life now would be as a coil of gold wire
threaded with turquoise, they said.
Nothing of dust or dross.
                    It rubbed off on him,
gave him kudos as he strutted
through the hot and viney hours:
My sweet daughter serves the Goddess.

But each night he staked out an illicit vantage point
over the holy blue cressets.
At his back, Shadow and Mountain, Lions there
in the clefts. Sometimes he longed for the burn
of their breath, his strong hands tearing thick manes,
his own exultant howling –
Better than watching the sickle moon
languidly downing her stark blade to his wrist.

If he heard the temple-snake rustle
his skin would contract, ready to evade
the slither that would surely come,
encircle his instep, his thigh –
Yet it stayed secret
and he named it Masculine, for its complicity.

In this dance the women's arms were white rods,
Lightning, he thought. Their feet sounded percussion
on the earth's drum the tension
flung up into electric air
attracting – or changing focus?
                    For the moths just fell,
wings immobilised, hundreds
of delicate beings, they
spiraled down gracefully, ran on the ground

shimmering for a while.
In the morning even the dust of them was gone.
Licked up by the greedy earth; or Snake.

Rattling on thinness of wrist and ankle
her serpentine bangles
echoed her babyhood arm's fat ring
about his heart; her moth-soft kiss
transfixed him. Now he refused to see
how she rouged her breasts
nor the avid strength of her hands
rending air.   She was
his own fine bloodline: *My daughter.*
Fathomless, she was
the chill pricking of hair on the nape of his neck.

A PRESENT FROM HELFORD

After the first days – the sun lulling,
sea-balm, light, the nard of pollen and salt
– after those days
the search for a gift to take him,
something to hold out with both hands:
'Look, this was the essence'

And what I remember still is the green estuary
and how in the dawn we took out a boat;
the sway as we waited, lines like antennae,
water, sky, lucent and silent,
the soft to and fro of the boat waiting
and the sea so utterly clear, pellucid.
Beneath us the restless careening shoals, each fish
almost escaping the flowing cloak of its shadow.
So nearly air this water, and air in my hands
spent like the sea.

Then the blaze –
blue and white running erratic waves
gulls' flight-paths crisscrossed on the wind
their displacement of air interlacing the cliffs
with the breakers, the granite and sand – even I.

I took my Father oysters fresh from their beds
in the bay. A dozen, packed in a neat pine box
and stencilled: Helford.
Open, it filled the prim town kitchen
with a memory of wildness, saltweed on the beach.
We neither of us knew how to eat them
so we stood mouths open, heads tipped back
holding the rough gaping shells like threats
above our throats –

then settled them gently back in their box.
I had never wanted to eat them
(poor wet mermaidy flesh alive in my mouth)
but I thought it something a man would do:
or a girl, intent on proving her new maturity.
                    Our shared repugnance
was one of our closest moments
there was nothing we needed to say.

And what I remember still today is the pale box,
knife and lemon on cream formica.
How then it seemed that we were the strong
and civilised ones, choosing to refuse
the barbarities of sophistication.

Gifts and essence,
a lattice laid down in silence. As oysters
milling their lives in the fathoms' tide-swell
hold the slow growth of the grain,
or ivory shells reveal the marks of their course,
travelling hones to a bare white thread
of spiral bone.

GREAT GRANDMOTHER SANG SOLOMON

My lay-preaching Grandfather's legacy of words
a God-blessed inheritance of Nile, Euphrates,
holy water words showering my infant head.
Myrrh breathed in Grandfather's beard, at his shoulder
rods broke into almond flowers.
He told me the terror of red Jordan
so my toes touched sandy pigments,
when the river rolled back its walls of gasping fish,
I saw their silvers
glint as ominous knives
and felt them thresh the turbulent mauve darkness
brinking the chanted Path; the Way a light-shaft
straight as a ruler.

Ezekiel, Rebecca, wolfish Cain with his bloody murder,
all these Grandfather received,
with parables and psalms
that stemmed in a fruitful harvest
from the grape-carved testered bed
where Great Grandmother in state
awaited the Coming.
She bore her seven children in the Faith
then closed her door at forty-five
to lie another half-life;
forty more years frozen
in the hope of cloistering with the Lord.

Her room is a night of crimson and walnut
sparked by the pearl of an inlaid box
or a sharp brass eye at the velvet's hem.
His childish shadow only slightly grazes the lamplight:
Surely she's lonely, shut away from my loving –

He inches into her sphere of linen, candle whiteness
she is singing Solomon, the Book at her breast:
O this is my beloved, he is white and ruddy,
chiefest among ten thousand, his mouth most sweet,
Yea, I am my beloved's and my beloved –
O he is mine. The burrs of her voice
unsettle him with love, go underneath his skin.
Words of God filling the soul with yearning:
hand over empty hand shaping a prayer.

APING THE MOTHER

Fruit in a jar with the taste of ashes,
the anger of bread, beaten and pounded:
women's hands must fill and refill
with the useful and warm things
                    – loaves, fishes
in parsley and babies
dying or growing
sliding away into other holdings,
slipping through scalded fingers.

Fists gripping hot needles draw out the blood
into fine lines of scarlet, silk
to knit skin and embroider
the ragged, wavering, secret edges
neat as a bed of pins.

I pin myself into the pattern,
the brown paper dress carefully scissored,
I pin the woman-shapes over me,
force their stiffness into curves and flowers;
they crackle, threaten like electricity,
they are the colour of brooding,,
they bruise on the mind.
Along my scarecrow arms I hang the jars
jewel-bright, lead-heavy,
berries of heart, lung, living and breathing
their ball-dress colours
trapped in the pantry glass.

Let the men make their chimeric castles,
their intricate constructions cocooned in the mass
of their own wordy history;
                    marvels in coldness

brilliant, dangerous to look at
while ice creeps, freezes, immobilises
tongues unable to lick into shape.

Oh Mother, there are words coming out of my fingers
and clambering all over the sky;
fiery words, first words, symbols of horses,
rosy crosses, green manifestoes, long poems in marble
to cut with a chisel, clay phrases
to stretch and mould with my thumb:
they are building up into something
vast as an anvil of thunder...

Go out with your gossamer net, my girl-child, quick
cram them back into their box, the curfew is coming;
time to feed crystalline fruit to the boys.

THE GLASS RITUAL

Time out of mind, the long-ago gift
of a green glass ball for 'Pisces'.
It glimmered with sea-light, storms and calms,
gracing the sheer polished heart of her mirror,
refracting the looping glass fictions
of Grandmother's beads
and her one real zircon, sharp as an idol's eye.

And as the glass pared her years
down and down towards the bone,
she reflected on her far-off, brief span
of credulity, remembered the terrified midnights
when the candle's ambivalent sheen
lustred the apple: the offering.
How she reeled out the ghostly words,
wanting, needing to catch only a glimpse
of his strange shadow
swimming the mirror's dark belladonna'd eye.
A lover, marked and certain
in her future's net.

Her room creaks dry as her empty hands,
old arid minutes shaping the atoms
of each chair, plate, framed face.
She knows no promises haunt in the speckled mirror–
but in the sea-lit deeps of the old glass ball
she curves and swells, fish-fat, fingers
tendrilled, floating pale kelp.
Repeating the ritual, she waits
for whatever may rise
from the green submarine space at her back.
She should have chosen the sea, long-ago.

CONNECTIONS

If I am aware, then the notes come;
I hear them – I suppose as bats do
or the broken-coated hound, whose eyes filter
something of earth's nature, whose eyes change
as he listens elsewhere. *Do you hear then?*
I ask him. *Is it Welsh rain coming to the garden,*
or something other? I only hear it through my hair,
the tips drink sound from silence.
Is this nectar then?
I imagine myself the humming-bird,
how this unchecked greenness would offer
hibiscus in the dog-rose, the wild sweetness
of some alien yellow juice
within the needled gooseberry or the stony pear.
The curlew bounces his song across the distance.
The hairs on my arm shudder with the wind.
My dog hackles uneasy, he thinks
I am too near to the raven as it rises, croaking,
too near to the muttering self-involved tree
experimenting its blossom beyond us.
No, I say. *Don't you see it?*
The buzzard disturbs us, he is painting a circle
such as the mouth of a net, about us.
We are all in it. All.

FARM WIFE

This September, the evenings – however visionary
with goldness – were given to paper
lying stark spilt milk on the kitchen oak.
She'd no mind for figures
so she'd stand at the yard gate
mooning, he said,
cursing and struggling
with the bloody inking of profit and loss.

From here, she could smell his machines,
the cold yellowness of bulldozer and crane
permeating the resins of nearer pine,
the sere lemon drivel of barley. At a mile she knew
their aura, the indifference
and brutality in them scoring over the land.
Oh, but he spoke of them as if they were his lovers,
their powers forcing his hand, flooding through him
as he rode and routed bracken edges, hedgerows,
gouts of black roots flung out in appeasing hands.
He played a kind of purse-lipped god out there:
I like things tidy, he said,
razing the kindness of orchids and winter aconite,
his iron, his weight, smoothing the mounds, the circles,
sucking the veins of the marshy places dry
for the corn's easy linear acres.
And now the papers came chittering into their hall.

At night he was lost and she knew it.
She was the drab ghost of trees lying beside him
rain running glistenings over her face.
He could not touch her; she was cold as stone,
frozen stone that burns you if you cleave.
She was going inward; into earth, into granite.

THE TRACTOR DRIVER

This is the worst phase of the ploughing;
from the huge field's centre he can see only
endless acres of cut brown earth
and blackened stubble. The green line of trees,
the hills and hedges are out of sight,
he is alone, small as a toy
on the rolling furrows, with only the sky to look at.
And that lies too close, enclosing him
in a stifling upturned bowl of blue hammered pewter,
its undulate rim defining the curve of the world.
His engine beats at the silence, reverberates under him,
beats at the drum of the cut brown earth.
This was yesterday and is tomorrow
on a thousand more acres.
It is the season of blackened stubble.

He goes home in darkness, headlights shaping the lane,
bleaching rabbits, a cat or two.
The day's work over, yet still
the pulse of the tractor shakes in his hand.
His fists tremble, he sees
new cuts, scabbed red lines over his knuckles,
the marks of another, small unimportant accident.
Nothing much – but he can't remember it happening
nor the sting of the pain.
His hands are telling him something.
He finds inexplicable bruises, black pinched nails,
little scratches, the purple-brown lice of blisters.
Day after day his big strong hands show him the marks
of his isolation, his tiredness and boredom.

But it's a living, these hard waking hours
spent unaware as a sleep-walker making his rounds.
It's a job – and there's a hundred men

CARIAD

Between hills plump as hens the summer road
speeds cars, bisects the bee-danced hedges;
a man, there, on the dangerous edge,
flaps and stutters, slurred feet swerving
in and out the verge, the blurred flowers.

His chin has fallen away from his stained face
with the weight of the whisky.
He is all weight, a big man in his bones,
dead heavy to have on our hands:
Where do you live? we ask him.
Over the hill, cariad,
over this little Welsh hill.

Inches away, isolate people
flash past us fast as a film
reeling the road up from the beaches.
He rocks to and fro, calls me *cariad,*
enters our car with confusion:
But you're English...

His farm lies in a sty of nettles.
In the bird echoes linger voices:
wife and daughter
tragedy ghosting quietly over the gate.
What is the answer, cariad?
Blue eyes washed by his own long rain
stare down the valley; the cuckoo trees,
the sepia river. *The finest fishing*
you'd be welcome...

The geography of his ruined heart
puzzles the wavering, changing boundaries,
the mirages of gentle friendly hills.

GREEN-GIRL, MILL-MAN

Colden Valley

His black mills and engine houses
show now in fractured sinews darking grass.
Once he fisted here, with stone as tight
as sutures on the push and flux of leafblade
light and water. Each stone
cut with his holy industrial note,
rasp in the throat of the mill-man:
bass cut, slabbed out, flat on the land.
Teeth in the neck he bridled the green-girl
scoldings of bud and bird, black smoke
hanging crape from her sycamores,
he held her, with reins of grim walls,
sunless walkways, his cock chimney rearing,
piercing the glade, her freshwater
silk on his harsh bricks and bones.
Soft touch: grist to his mill.

But now she has you, mill-man
in your hardness. Her roots wrap your pieces
in slow slow motion, tear you out,
break you. Her hair is combing itself
in a water-wrack right through the weeds,
she is sucking your stones inside
with her lips of pink balsam. Your angles
are bitten to roundness, your shorings
and banks made shale in her moody weathers.
Now she will ruin you, with her hounds
Moss and Lichen, Spore, Seed and Time.
She has set her trees on you like young dogs.

THE BOY MAKING THUNDER

The boy making Thunder
has whittled his stick from a slip of red yew,
set tin shivering, his drumbeat
shielding up over him – his bell-house.
            Birds spy him, fall silent,
uneasy they spy from the castlelling ivy.

His Thunder rolls itself out, a cloud of it
staining the thin muslin of silence,
insects' stitching, birds' seed-pearl voices.
The boy's Thundergame enters the afternoon
rooms of polished verbena, sets fringes whispering;
the cut flowers turn their heads,
shush petals together, weep
            bloodrose from the crystal vases.

Growing up, Thunder roars out over the roof,
jets across cool European skies, the boy
held in his frail barricade, his cockpit
fisted in clamour.
Trailing inflammatory tails like furies
Thunder writes on the wall of luminous air-space;
moves on,
makes clear beads dance on my mirror,
as if the glass sweated, as if today was hot.
            My kimono shivers, draws closer.

Prescience of flame thickens the air this stormy summer
dry blonde grass flickering, taut drumskin sky
for tinder. Birds huff their feathers
or fly mad shrieking.
            Early warnings? As if they knew,
expected, the lightning strike,
the flashing bolt from the blue.

SHOPPING COMPLEX, PLAZA, FOUNTAIN

Now at night, the earth is coffinned
by the buildings' box, all earth-breath
stopped: the breath the earthworms use,
beetles, millipedes, their strange frequencies
compressed to heavy dust. Nothing calls
or noses out, nothing bites,
        strings kisses.
Owls wide-berth the ledges, the fountain water
greens at its holding lip, promised spray
just white-dreamed lace   on the graph.

Nearby, in age-yellow bars
ghost stories are traced through the beer:
how they caught crayfish   in a jar of light;
watched coloured horse run
when the blowsey, smokey wind lifted them.
        And the secret: of a bed-soft bank
where everyone, once, in secret   lay
        grass-nested.

He flips his coin so high
it almost takes flight   but the fountain water
sucks it in like a miser:
This I shall have, and these cans and peels
your trash and treasure   all the same to me.
I shall hold what I have in the sump
in the sink of me, and one day
pay out for your drowned wishes:
give you the pencilled-in spray
bright as cellophane   gift-wrapping
concrete and sky-blue tile.

RED SCARF

On the way, a fox ran out jaunty
and red from the pheasant covers.
He danced
grinning all over
then snaked   quick fire
through fences   easy mesh.

In boxed   velvet shadows
Gran's foxfur hangs with chenille and jet
snarling wraith,
vitreous red gaze   spark
in the airless lamplight. Skin-ribbon
animal running supple through fingers.

She'd give me this as an heirloom
but I won't hazard my delicate neck
to it's satin-
lined sleekness. Let it coil,
with those tiny ivory teeth
nestle close   feel
the hot bite of wire, the noose tightening;
how the fire of my blood would run
quickly through needle serrations:
red scarf, warm to the skin –
the last red grin.

SEEDTIME

If I were to say that being here
I am also somewhere else;
that in my English fist I hold
the burning hallucinatory fibre of the desert,
the sign of the forest is on my palm
– blade and smoke, and the wave, tsunami
earth-coloured with fractions of lands
torn to papyri –   If then
I laid claim to bone-cut black and arid faces,
if I took to myself the extinct form
of the zoo's prize Madagascan lemur,
and the sunfish, embered globe lazing dead
in the Japanese driftnet – if
then I said: *These are my own seeds,*
I name them. I claim the whole corollary
of these fears. Would you then
see them in my verdant July garden,
discover their presence deep within
the sugared philadelphus or
the winding bee-sucked scarlet bean?
Would you see how the new sun
casts roseate shadows that worm blood-sinews
running out and through
the delicate veining of the orchid
and my milk-white hands?

ON THE ISLAND

FUGITIVE

The moon is fugitive this month
will not break the darkness, nor come near.

Her forehead pressed to the window-pane,
she feels its thinness – *it could shatter*!
too frail a barrier between
this house of shallow white brilliance
and the rain's blind sleeting.
Bound by the weather the tree's ferment,
roots clawed to the cliff; half of this garden
once slid in a chute to the jade Atlantic rollers:
violets salted in carragheen.

The third wild moonless night.
She has paced out her waiting
across billowing lawns; was warned where sea
sprayed up over the fuchsia's pendant red bells,
has seen the cold statue's nakedness
of white freckled shoulders, long flanks – but
ivy can sucker skin as easy as marble.
Alabaster limbs sprawled under leaves,
the tangle: black and white,
like one of those quick, quilty photos.

The cherubic clock in the hall
quarters the three, the four, her high heels
rap, pause, allow the silence
to smother the underdrum of her heartbeat,
the rain's pandemonium.
Damn moon, so late –
Her calendar is marked with the phases,
notations on certain nights. At home in the city
she glides through the warm achromatic rooms

silver fingers opening the shadows
of rosewood and steel. Here,
her timing is out.

Afternoons she sleeps, dreams of sea-rhythms
washing out measured months. She is out of her depths
must swim with the tide or drown,
a bloated, bloodless creature.
Waking, sea-sick, she feels her body
liquid and alive with secrets
that dart and pain like violent fish.

THE FISHERMAN

He was born to a sly dislocation of night and day,
cradled in noon-flood cabins
bobbing innocently over the shoals;
the purity of fish salting his milk,
his early opaque blue squint teased
by fish-scintillations.

Easier than words they taught him sea-weather,
the tunes of the engine and sail,
evasion and silence.
He learned the grip of the cliff's fierce ledges
and let their tenacious scent of slight roots
cool through his pores, absorbing a history of risk.

Thin legs running through childhood, eyes scanning
high as the shearwaters; his little senses
strung on a whistle, each grain of heather
corresponding to instinct bred on his radar skin.

Later, the marine currency
of slick, oil-wrapped secrets he handled alone
as cleanly as bass or mackerel.
An illicit magician, empowered and cunning enough
to go under the Ninth Wave and surface
far in the north; his long cargo
pricking the peace of a nation.

His only concern: with the black jut of tide,
the timber's obedience. And a dream
of Hy Brasil's beaches, the silky redhead
lying along his arm; the knarl of his thumb
turned deep in a strand of her foxy hair,
its colour alive as a brass line of sun
or tomorrow's horizon.

THE WATCHER

Her wolf-heart is hard, stone-silent;
she has chosen the side of the angels
can spit at danger, is slink and cunning
as the biggest fish in the bay.
She can see him coming, hindered
by moonlight and the hushing
waking of water – her net spiteful
as prison, tricksy as poacher's run.

Towards dawn she tasted again the salt wind,
as if the sun, breaking on a different beach
had ripened aromas from dulse and barnacle,
brought them in on the tide.
She still waited, her large stillness
inhuman, rockshape
under the breakwater blackness,
her fingers' tense oscillations
beaded by gravels of crabskin and shell,
as she listened, heard only
the slapping of water on wood attending
night's bleed into sunrise.

At last, the sea's empty screen dilates
to a dazzle of light; in the blinding
her shut eye dreams the familiar *oh such a one*
with his big hands to care and caress a mending
man she'd have none of the bully boy she'd too much
mind her books and prizes there, just so under
the curtain's chintz hem.
She moves doll-stiff in the daylight,
the raw wind's greyness biting her neck
without love. Beside her, the latest junking
of tar and plastic mars cockles, pearl-otters,
stains again the palimpsest sand.

She looks up as she leaves, sees the cliff
looming black metal, her watch-tower of steel;
and she in the dress of a high flyer,
nails full of gold-dust,
tilting the blazing search-light moon,
those righteous beams exposing the suck and swill
of the undertow's dirty new tide.

SILENT RUN

The strings of the sea-moon
set mercury jaws yawning the lips
of the black-mouth waves;
easy to think of fish flickering snake-tongues
in the tide, drifting poisons of cadmium,
radiant ores.
She sits close in to her polished self,
pitches her whispers under the engine's hum:
Is it always so calm?

In this metal light her lips are black fruit
white skin sheened to fish-glitter, woman of pearl.
She's trouble, he thought, aware of the words
crass fleshiness, their back-alley thrill
snaking sensations over the tension of muscles,
making his back sweat salt.
This is a month with no storms.
If you saw the day come up over the island
you'd be at peace. It's too pale a time
for anything but pleasure.

The inside of a shell, she said softly.
Sky stretched silk over the sea's glistening wetness.
The oyster, pearl and salt.

His hands kept their deftness, moon in his compass,
wind, water's white push on rocks.
If she smiled now, he would not see it.
The land neared, an unlit bulwark of darkness.
If he were the ferryman, this mercurial night,
what coin would she pay him?
Pieces of silver dissolving to water at dawn?
Fool's gold?   Or discs for his eyes
cut from perfect, reflecting germanium?

DARK HOUSES

Now ceased the dreams of drowning water.

As if she had come to this island
empty, light as a paper cup on the wave,
the big house, shut-eyed to the restless Atlantic,
soothed the journey out of her nerves,
offered some kind of seductive haven.
In her room an antique vase twined serpents
in blue glaze, emerald silk on the bed
made a sound that was utterly feminine.
He had left small gifts for her practised fingers;
netsuke, paste intaglios. And chrysoprase –
as if he knew it might cure her burning fever, or how
thieves once believed it made them invisible.
Stone of Pisces. She saw fish doubling back
in its cat-eye greenness, left it lying;
wore her own ring: the justice opal.
Preparing with skill for their first meeting
– black so to her hips, bare swerve of shoulders,
the flick of the small-boned gold-strapped wrist –
I am dressed to kill... moon white face in the mirror
listening, as briefly, she parted the blind
and looked out at the empty sea.

At night-time the movement of water deceives,
distances alter, islands hover in air,
slip out of their moorings and surface somewhere else,
whale-backed in a shoal of black rock.
Across the bay the house on the cliff
kept uneasy eyes on the ocean,
curtains unstilled by the faint sea-breath.
If she woke, it was always to startle at engines
or sail-creaks, rope and wood, ghost-boats

skulling out of her dreams; unseen freight of the dead
bound for the blest western islands.
I sleep too near, she thought, crystal-gazing
the moon trapped in her water-glass, seeing nothing;
turning, heaping the hot starchy pillows over the flood
of the tide's soft insistent coming and coming,
its half-wild moaning.
Soon she would find it unbearable,
would watch the bay from the window, nightdress
hugged tight over her knees as she scanned
the sea where no lights ever loaded the waves.

TOMORROW IS SOON

In still dark, light hanging at the point of change
he whistled a trick of wind
and stole the white yacht from her moorings.
Realised desire:
the rich man's pleasure ship in his hands,
with her own fey temper to try against time and tide.

This long shadowy hour before morning, he would seek
the place where the sea-goddess coiled,
an old serpent writhing the ocean wheel,
her mouth a bell of black pewter.
Here he would open his hold, let slip as an offering
the dead weight they had brought from the island,
let it spin down; alabaster fish
finding its five fathom grave.
Then fly south, without anchor into the sun.

This woman had seemed a cold siren. Coming sudden
out of the night, a dream – smooth moonstone skin
in the grassy dark. Yet she cried out
fiercer than shearwater's rising shrieks,
enough to wake the dead. (He had heard those birds
ensouled the damned in their hollow bones.) He smiled;
between them lay a shared act of violence, now
she was his fire to warm him against the future.
Soon, the wind will alter, tomorrow is soon.

The sea is a woman too, he told her.
She whispers to me her ways of wealth and weather,
forewarns me of moods when she might turn ugly
and raise her monstrous dripping mane
to whip the fulmars out of the sky. Those nights
I sleep in the lea of the wind.

But I'll show you her secrets: circling fingerprints
of current and vortex, slits and crannies
slashed from this wild obsidian rock.
My sea-lover shall hide us.

She watches his hands, assessing potential,
vitality. Hers are sweet as porcelain,
red nails skilled as the needle beaks of terns
swooping swift murder into the sea.
She watches faint phosphorescence glitter
as if something precious were spilt in the deep;
seeds of fire fuelling the difficult cyclic journeys
of unseen shoals. *I came with the salmon,*
drawn by my own inevitable moon-in-the-blood,
my lunacy. Now the tide turns, I return home, go east,
jink through the nets and snares beating the odds
for life. Tomorrow is soon.
After a while she saw the wide arch of a rock
looming black on the tarnished horizon.
A mouth she thought. *An entrance.*
I go down from here, enter the Underworld.

BEACHCOMBING AT DAWN

She coils him round, dreams him down to her secrets;
she is the crooning wave, he is helpless within her.
But she finds him only a pale ghost of a lover
and spits him out, leaves him for other predators.

Familiar now the different ways of morning:
sun brittling diamond horizons, Atlantic glory
burning through long citrine streamers,
or hunched angry weather sulking the cliffs
and queasy rollers. Mornings hidden
in rain's adamantine curtain.
She kept a spidery patience. Each separate tide
lifted sea-gifts to the beaches, to her cave-nets
and patrolled inlets. She watched and waited,
knew the detritus of dreams would come drifting in
with the salt-honed wood and cheap trashed plastic.

She found the bodies cradled in shallow water,
safe in the lea of the wind. Bleached faces
– mottled dark by savage contusions, sea-kisses –
floating under the surface as if silenced mouths
still drank deep of the wave's blue mandragora.

Days later, after the rule of law
had scoured and probed, made its harsh exposures,
she found an old ring knotted in wrack,
kept in a crack of rock; blue-bright seed,
fire-heart opal hinged to hold seawater secrets.
A Borgia ring, dispensing more elegant justice
than drowning. She thought of the wrecks in the bay,
sometimes these freak storms threw strange riches
to shore. Who had worn it? Were her hands like this,
roughened by water and weather, white half-moons
stark to her skin, nails bitten? She shrugged;
this was a prize, the reward of virtue and patience.
She snapped it shut, slid it onto her finger.

Acknowledgements

Some of these poems have appeared or are about to appear in the following magazines: *Poetry Wales, Distaff, Caliope, Borderlines, Celtic Dawn, London Magazine, New Prospects, New Welsh Review, Out of Bounds* and *Orbis*.